PENGUIN BOOKS

UNMASTERED

Katherine Angel is a writer and academic. Her writing has appeared in the *Independent*, *Prospect*, the *New Statesman*, *Aeon*, and *Five Dials*. She studied at Cambridge and Harvard universities, has a PhD from Cambridge, and after a fellowship at the University of Warwick, currently holds a research fellowship at Queen Mary, University of London.

Unmastered

A Book On Desire, Most Difficult To Tell

Katherine Angel

PENGUIN BOOKS

PENGUIN BOOKS

Published by the Penguin Group
Penguin Books Ltd, 80 Strand, London WC2R ORL, England
Penguin Group (USA) Inc., 375 Hudson Street, New York, New York 10014, USA
Penguin Group (Canada), 90 Eglinton Avenue East, Suite 700, Toronto, Ontario, Canada M4P 2Y3
(a division of Pearson Penguin Canada Inc.)
Penguin Ireland, 25 St Stephen's Green, Dublin 2, Ireland (a division of Penguin Books Ltd)
Penguin Group (Australia), 707 Collins Street, Melbourne, Victoria 3008, Australia
(a division of Pearson Australia Group Pty Ltd)
Penguin Books India Pvt Ltd, 11 Community Centre, Panchsheel Park, New Delhi – 110 017, India
Penguin Group (NZ), 67 Apollo Drive, Rosedale, Auckland 0632, New Zealand
(a division of Pearson New Zealand Ltd)
Penguin Books (South Africa) (Pty) Ltd, Block D, Rosebank Office Park, 181 Jan Smuts Avenue,
Parktown North, Gauteng 2193, South Africa

Penguin Books Ltd, Registered Offices: 80 Strand, London WC2R ORL, England

www.penguin.com

First published by Allen Lane 2012
Published in Penguin Books 2014
1

Copyright © Katherine Angel, 2012

Set in Scala Pro
Typeset by Palimpsest Book Production Ltd, Falkirk, Stirlingshire
Printed in Great Britian by Clays Ltd, St Ives plc

978–0–718–19477–2

www.greenpenguin.co.uk

Penguin Books is committed to a sustainable
future for our business, our readers and our planet.
This book is made from Forest Stewardship
Council™ certified paper.

For Rachel

One after another, she, Lily, Augustus Carmichael, must feel, our apparitions, the things you know us by, are simply childish. Beneath it is all dark, it is all spreading, it is unfathomably deep; but now and again we rise to the surface and that is what you see us by.

Virginia Woolf, *To the Lighthouse*

To Spend Oneself, To Gamble Oneself

1. Nearly ten years ago, in that sweltering summer, that heatwave summer, when to walk just half a mile meant a sticky sheen of sweat, I developed a phobia of moths.

I had never liked them, my nervousness shaped no doubt by my mother's fear of the things. Her brother used to breed huge African specimens in their East Anglia home; they would fly up at her, startled, out of her shoes, her bedclothes. And then there was a teenage summer spent in a Gothic pile in France, where hordes of angry bees rattled behind the chimney, and disconcerting noises-off unsettled the most rational of family and guests. Fat armies of sated flies and flotillas of dark, wide moths appeared every night in a room in which my sister eventually refused to sleep.

When the stay was over – but only then – we speculated giddily about dead bodies under floorboards.

So far, so manageable. But when that heatwave brought fatter, more alien moths to a tiny university town where I was deeply in love, and caught in the headlights of a PhD, dislike burgeoned into something else: an all-consuming terror whenever one would flap and flutter into view. Its blurry agitation would have me darting across a room before I knew what I was doing. Once, I leapt out of a shower in panic as one frantically ricocheted around the folds of a curtain. Out like a shot, I stood dripping shampoo on the hall carpet. The worst prospect: a moth sticking itself to my wet skin. It might disintegrate. A wing would be detached from a body; several different bits of moth might be stuck to me.

Dead, dismembered moth.

I went to a friend next door to rinse my hair.

There was a phase of nervously checking, at arm's length, the curtains in my bedroom before sleep, poised to sprint from the scene should one rise from the lurid floral pattern. The pleasure of open windows on summer evenings was fraught with danger: those bloody things, drawn to the light. Static, embracing a wall, they were almost worse, for they would inevitably move, taking disorganized, fitful flight. And when they were immobile one could see, if one dared look, their dreadful texture, their vile components.

I dreamt, once, of one pinning me down on the stone slabs of a suburban garden. It settled softly on me, trapping me under its insect blanket.

1. Good loving can be fortuitous; partly a question of timing.
    A few years ago, emerging from a subterranean place –
    the lifting away of unhappiness – up, up, away! – a balloon
    released – I unfurled myself, out of a paralysis of thought,
    feeling, memory.

    I was purring.

    And then I met him. That first night: me climbing on to
    the back of his Vespa, he leaning back to grab my bare,
    uncertain legs, placing them on the rests. On his sofa, we
    unwrapped each other; and then he stood up, lifting me
    with him, carried me next door and flung me onto the
    bed.

    I was awash with pleasure.

    I was a wisp, and I was free.

2.   He was silent; I was chatty.

One night, as early morning light grew outside and we lay entangled, a blur of skin and limbs and mouths, I spoke dreamily of how I loved his big frame towering over me during sex; how much I loved his powerful arms around my neck while he came into me from behind; how I loved feeling the strength of him as he fucked me – yes, as *he* fucked *me*, because – let's not be coy, or disingenuous – that is definitely what was happening.

I trailed off in my reverie. He looked at me, shifting his head back as if to get a clearer view, and said, You're not really a feminist, are you?

I laughed.

I didn't explain why.

1. I like to look at pornography. Well, certain kinds of pornography.

   It probably doesn't count as pornography for many people. Much of it is quiet, hushed – often photographs.

3. What I like – or what I like to look at, which may not be the same thing – is the kind of classy kink that seems just distant enough from the grimy associations of porn ('porn', not 'pornography') that I feel able to walk the tightrope of sheer instrumental lust without cringing. Stylized bodies, full of knowing and play; highly aestheticized, even down to the disavowal of that aesthetic. Talented, witty photographers – playful, full of postmodern intertextuality!

This knowing, ironic aesthetic accomplishes a neat function: it doesn't *feel* like porn. Or like how I think porn should feel, which is to say: misogynistic, coercive, tacky.

4. But misogynistic, coercive, tacky porn isn't necessarily unerotic – it just depends what you mean by erotic. These butch, taciturn men and shiny tottering women, in their bleakly naff trysts – they make me uncomfortable. They make me squirm with laughter, they make me cover my eyes, sometimes they offend me. There is something deathly, joyless in their performances. They leave me feeling vaguely deflated, slightly melancholic – a feeling akin, perhaps, to the desolation, the intense pang of aloneness, that male friends and lovers have sometimes described experiencing after orgasm alone or with someone they do not love.

1. I like to imagine, to fantasize, him orchestrating me –
    and, well, orchestrating others around me. He is telling
    them what to do. No part of me is unattended. He is
    ensuring that all the things I want when I am with him
    – all together in an impossible overlap, for he has only got
    two hands – are possible. Telling them all what I like, and
    how, and why.

2.   He is not afraid of my desire, of its depths, its lengths.

3.   He doesn't know of his orchestrating role, of his regular outings in my head, when I am alone, when he is not in my bed.

      There is much I do not say.

1. What is it to define, or even to know, our desires – to identify which are our own, and which result from a kind of porousness?

   There is danger, as well as social capital, in this porousness, in intuiting the other's desire, and conflating it with one's own – as Virginia Woolf well knew. 'Killing the Angel in the House', she wrote, was 'part of the occupation of a woman writer'. The violence was necessary; without it, that Angel – sympathetic, charming, unselfish ('if there was chicken, she took the leg; if there was a draught, she sat in it') – 'would have plucked the heart out of my writing'.

2. This porousness: Susan Sontag grappled with it in her diaries: the 'compulsion to be what the other person wants'. She called it X, being Xy; 'the scourge'; not knowing what your feelings are, and 'liking being agreeable'. A deference to the other, to the point of not knowing that you have incorporated the other, in your very vacillation, your charm, your pliability, your politeness.

Words Words Words:
Or, To Marry A King?

1. Talking dirty. We're told we should do it. *Cosmo* urges us to do it. Countless sexperts, and even the NHS, tell us to do it. It's the mark of liberated modern lovers – where the era of communication valorized above all else meets the era of post-feminist performance.

   Fuck me. Oh yes, fuck me. I love it when you fuck me. You're so hard, you're so big. Oh I'm imagining you're behind me, you're spanking me, you've got my hair in your hands, I'm screaming ...

3.   There are many audiences for these words. Myself. My mother-feminism. And the lover; the man; The Man, the masculine. Yes, you are my big man, fucking me. Yes, you're so big, so hard. Yes, you are everything you feel under pressure to be. I am not disappointed! You know that deep well of fear that flickers in your eyes? I can see it, I can feel it, and I am telling you that it does not exist. I am pouring myself into that well; I block it up with my sympathy, my empathy, my acute feeling for your anxiety.

I am proof of your masculinity, of your endless potency.

I must reassure you. This is what I must do.

4.   Carolyn Steedman describes staying at school late one
evening as a child, without telling her mother:

'She was waiting on the doorstep: I withered, there was
nothing I could say. She'd wanted me to go down the road
to fetch a bunch of watercress for tea, and I ought to have
known she couldn't go, couldn't leave my sister. I fell into
the dark place of her displeasure, the sinking feeling of
descent. She wasn't like my grandmother, didn't go out
enjoying herself; and neither should I.'

Then: 'In this way, you come to know that you are not
quite yourself, but someone else.'

5.   She is talking about a mother; I am talking about a lover.
      A lover, in relation to whom I 'take on the burden of being
      good', of 'the capacity to know exactly how someone else is
      feeling'.

      I may be the whore in the bedroom, but I am still the
      Angel in the House. If there is a draught, I sit in it. If
      there is chicken, I am taking the leg.

1. When the doing is dominated by speaking, when there are too many words words words, it is because, in fact, you are somehow not enough. By which I mean that you do not *feel* yourself to be enough; and that feeling makes you shrink, in your eyes and mine.

   The frenzy of words: I feel your fear, and I struggle to protect it from the truth.

2. As girls, wrote Susie Orbach, we learn that 'if there is a game between the sexes in which one side has to lose, we had better make sure we are the losers.' Or we had better make sure that you, the man, are not the loser – or do not feel that you *could* lose. Competition must be foreclosed. I must protect you from your own fear.

3. The talking – all that feverish speak – is also a way to protect *myself* from the truth, and to take bellows to the fire. In reassuring you, I am also reassuring myself, because sometimes I need to goad my desire along. And because sometimes I need to make you bigger.

   Talking fills you up, fills me up, fills us up.

4.   It is also a way to make you represent something, culturally, that my femininity does not. I want to feel your decisiveness, your force. In lieu, perhaps, of feeling my own. I want to feel your capacity to resist me, your unaccommodatingness. Because otherwise you will not be A Man in the eyes of the world.

Eyes which are, of course, also mine.

6.   For Sontag, X – this thing she could not find words for
– was the desire to place oneself 'under the other's
protection'.

Is this what I desire? The king's protection? Perhaps. If
so, I foster it by protecting the king, by foreclosing the
possibility that I don't desire him, by hiding his fear from
himself. Inflating him – engorging him – with my
facilitating, accommodating desire.

7. Fuck me. Yes, fuck me!

1.   Words. Words. Words.

I want more silence.

With him I am quieter. I am also noisy, it's true, because when he is inside me, when he handles me, it's a shock – a deep, juddering pleasure, a ferry's heavy murmur.

But it's also a release, an arrival. And somewhere in myself I am quieter. I rest somewhere more peaceful. I have sunk down into my self, into my desire. I have become a body.

I have sounds, but I have fewer words.

2.   I don't remember what we did, or what we said, that first
night – or was it a day? I just remember the feeling of
being met, of being encountered; of meeting, of
encountering. Of contact, resistance, presence.

The wordless pleasure of simply feeling his warmth near
me; of looking at him; of lying there, together, distinct,
almost unconcerned. We chatted – we laughed – we dozed
– I sang – and he said, softly, not really to me, almost to
himself: I love fucking you.

It was an afterthought. It wasn't the main act. Or even an
act at all.

3.   A few days later, I am thinking of him more, again. I want
     to taste him; to seek solace in his warm, long body. I want
     to swim over to Friday, to him, to that tapas bar in Soho. I
     am in the waters, and when I fall asleep at night I feel
     myself cutting through their coolness, propelled by my
     desire.

     I will rise up out of the water and kiss him.

4. Months earlier, he sat in the living room on a slow, dozy Sunday, and our almost-still-kitten mooned up to him, enchanted. She rubbed her nose on his legs, pressing herself insistently into him. He picked her up in his elegant hands and she became long – an unravelled, yielding rope of cat. She dangled from his hands, eyes half closed.

I feel like Lottie, I said, once we had found a way to one another. You could take me by the scruff of the neck.

1. There are things that are hard to say. To say out loud, or to say to oneself. An imagined audience looms: a forbidding aunt, perhaps, with a wagging finger, a stern eye – peering over a lorgnette, even. A hypostasized mother, self-contained, watching in quiet consternation as I gesture and laugh and blink and pout and wrinkle my forehead in thought.

2. 'The woman,' writes Havelock Ellis, 'admires the male's force; she even wishes herself to be forced to the things that she altogether desires.' He must cultivate force, but be able to divine the moments when it is 'no longer force because his own will is his partner's will'.

All this 'at the very moment when his emotions are least under control'.

'We need scarcely be surprised,' Ellis concluded, 'that of the myriads who embark on the sea of love, so few women, so very few men, come safely into port.'

1.   Coming safely into port.

Sitting astride him, his hands on me.

These are lovely, he says. I laugh.

What is happening there, in that laugh? So many things.
A rush of glee, of delight. It is *me* he likes, *my* breasts. He
likes breasts, of course, and he likes mine – these very
ones, here, that he is playing with. The moments of doubt
– dispelled by a beautiful boy admiring me, pressing,
moving, pinching me.

2.   This is a thing that is hard to say.

3.   These are lovely. There is something worldly, too, and
      entitled, to that phrase. He has been around; he is a lover;
      he loves. He knows what he likes, and he likes me, mine.
      The quiet triumph! The thrill to be reminded, in those
      three throwaway words, that he happens to like my
      breasts, but could not. The flicker of insecurity it triggers.
      We happen to be here, now – and right now he is
      admiring my breasts.

4.   The faintest suggestion that he is admiring a *part* of me.
      That he is looking at, and liking, parts of me. The
      flickering shadow of appraisal, of the pornographic gaze;
      the feeling of disposability – replaceability. Do the various
      bits of me please him?

      I am unsettled, discomforted, excited.

6.   I pull off his shirt: a ripple of pleasure. He is beautiful; his chest, his shoulders. When I unbutton his trousers, and pull out his cock, another scattering of feelings – a shudder, almost. It is beautiful. It unnerves me, in its gorgeous attentiveness. The contact: always tremulous, a little alarming; will I understand it? These creatures, so heavy, a world unto themselves.

7.   It is beautiful. I love feeling hooked on it, aloft, brought into some dark, unfathomable place of myself. I love feeling my mouth on it, around it. I love feeling the weight of it, the weight of him.

I long – like the women in the 'love poetry of every age' – to be 'weighed down by the man's body'.

Love poetry written largely by men. No matter: I long to be weighed down by the man's body.

8. On the phone, one night, he tells me he is longing to feel my weight on him. 'The heaviest of burdens,' writes Kundera, is 'simultaneously an image of life's most intense fulfilment. The heavier the burden, the closer our lives come to the earth, the more real and truthful they become.'

1.   I ask him if he would tie me up.

Yes, he says, But when you don't ask me.

1.   He doesn't say much, but what he does say is thrilling. I
don't think he means it to be, which helps.

I love this thing in there, he says, gesturing down.

The way he says it: kind of off-handedly, absent-mindedly;
as if part of him is elsewhere. I don't think he really cares
how it sounds. He is not aiming at anything; at being
erotic, or erotically disrespectful. Nothing.

He is not really saying it for me.

2.   His sense of entitlement, to this, to me, to pleasure.

Entitlement: what women find harder to claim, what men have in spades, and so easily shades into aggression, into violence.

3. I love this thing in there.

    I shudder and laugh; this phrase delights me.

    My laughter amuses him. We laugh a lot: in bed, in the
    kitchen, on the phone. His laugh is a deep staccato,
    almost spoken. I feel it in my belly. It triggers mine; that
    triggers his. Before long, we are a festival of laughter.

4.   He knows I am writing about sex. On the phone, on a day when I am at a desk in London and he is by a fire somewhere, I tell him I have written a lot today. He says, You know, I have just now put these things together: you and I have sex, and you are writing about sex. He laughs – a wide open laugh. I say, Well, we could stop having sex while I write all this. Is there another option? he asks. Well, no, I say, you just have to feel the fear.

And then, softly, in another register: I miss all that, he says.

5.   He wants his own words.

He has his own words.

1.   He is above me. He dips his head to kiss my neck; and suddenly, before me, stark in my field of vision, is his spine: articulated, hard, precise. I gasp. The vertebrae pushing at his skin: so separate, so much distance between them. His head bowed, his shoulder blades rise up, jut out – and for a moment I am terrified, and thrilled – I feel something will burst out of his skin – wings – he will become an angel, a swan.

2.	I don't remember what we do. A wash, a smudge of memory – memory of time stretched, unstructured, no time. I remember feeling so heavily happy, so drowsily arrived. That I could feel my organs, their ripeness, their contentment.

3.	I want my desire to be exhausted.

4. Sex, said Sontag – 'unlike writing a book, making a career, raising a child' – is 'not a project'.

    Sex 'consumes itself each day. There are no promises, no goals, nothing postponed. It is not an accumulation.'

5. My head is on his thigh, his hand is on my belly. He strokes my hair and we admire each other in the darkening light, the soft, porous night.

6.   His hunger feeds me. We meet, and live that hunger – his, mine, ours – and afterwards, we are ashes. We are the good Zen bonfire: we have left no traces.

We have burnt ourselves completely.

1. At times, in the past, I have felt unmet, unmatched. Hungry.

   Restless, like the cat when we put her on soft food for a week, and she paced the room, gnawing at the furniture, pressing her teeth into hard surfaces.

2. Where to put that hunger?

   In a relationship where my drive, my ambition, made me too loud, and upset our economy – an economy I nonetheless longed to preserve – I turned the volume down on myself; I became less.

5. But in an Xy world, in the social world, where it is the social that we want – fine clothes, a house, to marry a king – better to have a pleasing manner, to be good, to be liked by each in turn, than be like Nahum Glatzer, who would 'come to Brandeis faculty parties, say at some point in the evening that he would leave at 10:00, and at exactly 10 would get up + no matter what anyone said would leave. Of course, no one usually said anything – just because he looked like a man who was doing what he wanted to do, who intended to do it, *who wasn't in the least tempted to do otherwise.*'

'There's the secret. Then no one can tempt you.'

6. Let the boy win at tennis!

1. In the realm of the body, it was pain that let the boy win at tennis. My desire – for us, for life, for everything – showed him up. And so it made excuses for itself. It chased itself out of the room – but on the way, it got stuck under my skin, my bone, my muscle.

2. The 'rhapsody, the self-surrender' that Lily Briscoe sees 'on so many women's faces': the 'rapture of sympathy'. James Ramsay sees it too: 'they look down, at their knitting or something. Then suddenly they look up.'

3. The pain contained me. It allowed me to stay still, to protect what we had.

I could still be good. I wanted to be good!

For I am nothing if not companionable. I like to keep them company, these ambivalent, suffering men.

4. The pain eventually went. But the hunger, the leftover; where could it go?

Elsewhere, when I found myself looking out of the frame – where he needed me to be less, and I wanted him to be more – I both made myself smaller, and turned myself up, so as to turn him up too.

I filled him up with my desire. I took bellows to the fire.

5.   Give me more. Be more! Satisfy me.

       Here, let me help you. We will stage a play together.

6.   Fuck me. Yes, fuck me!

(The Skill First) To Make Her Desire

1. He holds his own desire, and inhabits it. He takes up his space fully. Quiet, in a room, I can still hear him, his presence.

2. I am admiring his back; his shoulder blades; his wings. Look, I say, you have wings. He smiles; I have a tail, too, he says. I touch his coccyx; the hard circle of it at the end of his long spine.

3.   He is holding my waist, tenderly but with insistence. He pushes himself deeper into me. Gradually, we are frenetic. I don't remember what we are doing, exactly. Nothing happens in sequences; nothing is discrete.

What I remember is that an image inserts itself, suddenly, of him hitting me. Of him, yes, hitting me. It remains unclear; what do I mean? Being slapped? I don't think so. Punched? Surely not. Somewhere between the two, perhaps. The content has blurred edges, but the feeling is precise.

I want him to do something like hitting. Something – something – that would stop me in my tracks.

I want to say crazy stuff, I whisper. He says, Tell me.

But I don't; I hold back.

4. Sometimes, in talk, we explore. It is all wide open – a
    continent of desire. But he too knows the fears, the risks;
    the symbol that becomes real, the real that becomes
    symbol. The metaphors we love by.

5. When he grabs my hair, when he presses my throat, when he holds my hands down, I know – because I feel – that this is pitch perfect. It is pitch perfect because I can feel his tenderness, his humility, in this exploring, this wading into the sea together.

6.   I can feel his love. Sometimes I think I can taste it.

It hums around me, even while he remains distinct, self-possessed, contained. I feel it when we walk in silence along the canal, peering into the riverboats. I feel it when we're in a roomful of friends, eating roast lamb, and he puts a hand, a gentle hand, on the small of my back. I feel it on the phone, in exchanges and in silences – warm, pulsating silences, hearing each other's breathing. I feel it when we stir in sleep. And I feel it when we are on the rugged tracks of desire, careering towards something, pitching this way and that, threatening to tip over any moment; when his hands are in my hair, and he is inside me, and I am biting him, and we are all teeth and claws and wings.

1. In these moments, when we are seen, revealed as ferocious, and also vulnerable – unmastered – I think of a monster thrashing out of a lake, an arc of splash in its tail's wake.

2. 'It is fatal,' wrote Woolf, 'to be a man or woman pure and simple.'

3. Must I either take, or be taken?

   Must I either do, or be done?

4.	He has it just right, somehow. And I could never explain it to anyone.

There are no rules. Nothing fits all. We step out, haltingly, into the shifting sands of our own desire, our own opaque excitement.

1.	We are lying, afterwards, in a hot heavy heap. I tell him about the image, the feeling. He is calm, curious, steady. Nothing ruffles him, his long, sleek feathers. Do you think you want me to do that, he asks, or do you like just to imagine it? I think I probably don't. No, probably not.

	We turn it over. We let it remain a question.

2.	'My mother,' wrote Sontag, 'improved her manners by losing her appetite.'

4. I dreamt, once, of being alone in a large round room; I could see nothing, but I could feel an animal, a large, musky animal, circling around me. It sought me out, insistent, its nostrils flaring. Its hot breath warming the air; the hairs on my neck rising, my pupils dilating. It was there, but I couldn't see it.

I couldn't see it, but it was there.

More Gone

1. We are at home, listening to songs and undressing each other. We have been in the pub, his hand, again, on the small of my back as we laugh with friends.

The rush of feelings. The mounting wanting.

I spend a long time, eyes closed, tracing his shoulder blades. He spends a long time tracing my mouth. I want to be above him. I want to lower myself down, and envelop him; I want to lose myself, and – yes, I guess – fuck him.

2.   'I guess': a little shrug, eyes averted. 'I want to fuck him': I
      step to the side of that phrase. It sits in my mind in
      embarrassed, inverted commas.

      Fucking him. I feel there is something posturing,
      fraudulent, about it. I can't really fuck him, not the way he
      fucks me. Not really. If I say it, I am standing outside
      myself; I feel I am playing at something. Pretending to
      cheer on a football team, clutching a beer, wearing a red
      shirt that does not belong to me. Yeah! Come on! Yeah!

4. But so – we walk up the stairs, and I am imagining him under me; I'm having my way, holding his hands down, angling myself just right. And yet, I notice, I am tucking these desires away, putting them on hold. I am nudging these desires – to what? fuck? dominate? be on top? – round the back of the bed, letting them wait their turn. Surely this man – surely The Man – will not be fully satisfied if I take control; surely he needs to be full-on-fucking me to be replete, to have his hunger sated?

6.   Is this a compulsion to be what the other person wants? Am I sitting in the draught, taking the leg? Am I not quite myself, but someone else?

7.   Not exactly, or not only. It may be a compulsion to be what I *think* he must want, given that he is A Man. A compulsion to make him what we both need him to be.

     I lock him into his masculinity. I am anxious to protect it, for it pains me, it pains my femininity, to see it fragmented.

8.   I travel in a loop of gender.

     I was weaned on this – the hypostasized, brutal man; the
     yielding, deferring woman.

9.   So, by the way, were you.

10. Sometimes, he tells me, he intends to kiss me briefly, a quick little kiss, but cannot do it; before he knows it, the kiss is deep and heavy, and we are pulled in, into the undertow.

I imagine that nothing touches him. I buy the script; the script that says, because he is A Man he is safe, he is protected. That it is I, the woman – the girl – who is vulnerable and fragile. But where I, sometimes, have to stop, brought up short by a feeling of dissociation, he too has to retreat, halt, reground.

Sometimes it is *me* who is going too fast, and he too is brought to the brink, the brink of himself.

11.   My man. This man. The Man. No wonder, sighs Ellis, that
      'so few women, so very few men' – the anguish in that
      very! – 'come safely into port'.

12.   Coming safely into port.

      He puts down anchor in me, and finds his masculinity
      there.

      I put down anchor in him, in his masculinity, and find my
      femininity there.

13. A port: a place to rest. A place also to traverse, to pass through.

Putting down anchor, but only for a while.

1. I am sometimes afraid of the pleasure that comes from being on top. I am afraid because it is deeper, rageful, guttural.

    I am afraid of becoming a man. All muscle, fur, eruption.

    I am afraid of repelling with my desire.

2. It is fatal to be a man or woman pure and simple.

3.   I tell him, once, that I am a little afraid.

Let it come, he says, as I veer towards it, Let it come.

1. When I was a teenager, when I was small, and feeling desire – an amorphous lust, targeted at no one particular thing, and perhaps in fact targeted at myself – I wondered: where were the hungry women?

2. My mother and I are listening to the radio. We are
    probably washing up – she washes and I dry. I am,
    perhaps, fifteen. A woman – what could this programme
    have been? – is railing against oral sex, the political
    indignity of giving it. She never did, and she never would.

    My mother looks at me. There is a stillness, and then she
    says, Well she doesn't know what she's missing, then!

    We erupt in laughter; raucous, unladylike laughter. And
    then reddening cheeks, averted eyes.

3.   Mostly there were no hungry women – except those hungry for the food they forbid themselves.

     An attenuated hungry voice.

4.   I was hungry, and excited, and the words I would have put this into, had I felt the urge – the words I still put this into – are these:

     I feel like a man.

5. Man in drag, says Rachel. The man in drag who lives in the cupboard, the cupboard where we store our unconscious, and from which we retrieve clothes to un-drag ourselves.

1. The hungry female voice – unpathologized –
    unproblematized – sometimes one finds it – distorted,
    refracted, diffused, yes, through a fantasy of what men
    are, of what they can give, and of what they can control, of
    what they can contain, a fantasy that distances fear, fear of
    this hunger that is both exciting and threatening –
    nonetheless, one sometimes finds it – in pornography.

2.   When he is spent, and even if she has come, she can be satisfied anew. She can come again, can clamber out of bed in search of another.

He is dispensable. You, good sir, are not enough.

The pornographic woman: endlessly fucked and fuckable. This woman – endlessly stimulable, endlessly desiring – is what he tries to tame. He tries to insert himself into that endless loop of arousal and desire, of hunger and satiation. It is he who satisfies her, again, again, again. He. His cock. His.

She is also, then, the image of him; the fantasy image of he who can go on for ever, who is never disappointing. Always erect. Always at the ready. Always full of satisfaction.

She – this figure – is what he feels he himself should be.

1.   Sometimes when he fucks me, I feel I am fucking myself.

I feel I know what it is like to be a man. What it is like managing a penis, moving it around when it is sleepy – a head flopping forward on a lolling tube train; wincing when a hair gets caught under foreskin; holding it deep down at its base when it is full and glorious, and it rises yet more, arching, trying to take flight.

I feel I know that feeling.

2. I imagine sex with her – or is it me? – through his eyes. I see myself as he might.

I allow myself desire for her through my desire for him.

3. But what is it that anyone is excited by when they do, when they watch, when they imagine? When a paint-spattered shirt, a precarious high heel, catches their eye?

4. When I do, when I look, when I imagine, there is a scattering, a diffusion of perspectives. A recalibration of my centre of gravity.

    Sometimes I am just a mouth. Sometimes just a hand. Now I am that tongue; now I am that fold. Sometimes, I am just a feeling. Sometimes just skin.

5.   I am doing, and I am done.

      I am going, and I am gone.

1.   Longing: plaintive, cloying.

     Voracious: preying mantis.

     Promiscuous: unnatural.

     Rapacious: materialist, gold-digger.

2.   I want my own words.

3. I am so fucking hungry!

1. Back then, listening to the radio, I feel my mother's desire to let me explore, to let me experience pleasure. But I can also feel her fear, her anxiety. Her desire to look away, to cover her ears, to cut off my hair.

   Now, in a living room, on a spring day, I have cooked lamb and lentils, and made lemon ice cream, for the people I love. Somebody – provocative – asks my parents, So how much do you know about Katherine's book?

   And my mother, though she can be a little shy – birdlike, alert in her movements – is now in her element, and she tells a story. We tell this story together; we stand in the limelight, we play for our audience, this room full of love, ages, stages. We take it in turns, we pass it back and forth. The story goes like this:

   We are on the phone. I mention the writing, and she says, I'm very curious, Katherine, to know what this book is about. I say, half-parodying myself, but half not: Well, it's about, you know – S-E-X.

   Quick as a flash, alarmed, unsettled, she says, Oh it's not, is it? I think she, too, is half-playing, half not. Sort of, yes, I say. And then, again, sending myself up, but not entirely: Will you still love me?

2.   She laughs. We laugh. I don't remember her answer.

      We are joking, but we are both a little afraid.

3. After coming one morning – so strong – I cry. Sometimes it makes me cry.

I say, Sorry, sorry; he says, Don't apologize sweetheart. He holds me. He asks, softly, curious, gentle, What is it you're feeling? And I say, tears streaming, I feel like I'm dangled over the edge of a cliff.

The edge of a cliff!

He says, I'm here, I'm holding you. I've got you. His arm is under me, around my waist. I've got you.

Safe Words: Or, Quickly, Kindly

1.   Pleasure, wrote Foucault – pleasure in the truth of pleasure – is sustained, 'but not without trembling a little', by the obligation of truth. By the formidable 'pleasure of analysis'; the pleasures and obligations of confession.

'Why,' he asked, 'do we say, with so much passion and so much resentment, that we are repressed?'

'What led us to show, ostentatiously, that sex is something we hide?'

2.   All this telling, all this showing!

I display. I confess. To whom? The companions of a life so
far, perhaps – the allies, their visions and lights, showing
the way.

My people.

3. This gesture. I am thumbing my nose – at what?

   The pleasures of transgression. Fuck you.

4. We assemble – *on bricole* – our beliefs from myriad elements, stones we pick up on a beach, as we grow into our lives.

1. I think today is the day when I will tie you up, he says.

   He takes his belt, winds it around my wrists. I think of things I have read, Rule Number 5 in some article or other: You Have To Have A Safe Word.

   But I like there being no words! No method. No rules. I don't like taking instruction.

2. There is utter silence between us; just feelings of rupture.

   I am trying to break through the fabric, the fabric of things.

3.   Afterwards, he undoes the belt. We have some lunch and go for a walk.

Later, back at mine, we drink tea with Rachel, who has made a rhubarb cake and macaroons.

The sun is out. It is spring.

1.   What I love: that one day I said, I'd like you to tie me up.
       And then one day he did.

       He didn't check in, he didn't confirm that I did, in fact,
       want what I had said I wanted. He assumed that since I
       had said it, I had meant it. He assumed that I had spoken
       the truth about my desire.

3.   I haven't always taken myself at my word. I have
      sometimes – often – said things I didn't mean. A gesture
      of largesse, of being OK with something – not so much in
      bed, but in the mundane things of life. Yes, let's see that
      film. No, really, it's fine. Yes, I'll have another glass of
      wine.

      Gestures that are a compensation for a feeling of guilt;
      guilt about standing by one's own desires, about naming
      them, and about even feeling them.

      Gestures that come from a certain kind of love: love that
      'cuts the tendons of the will'.

5. X, said Sontag: the compulsion to be what the other person wants. The scourge: not knowing what your feelings are; liking being agreeable.

6. I don't want to merge, to know everything, to spend endless default time. I don't want your bright light shining on me, the light that illuminates us both.

You get on so well! You endorse, you support. You affirm one another in an endless maze of deflection. But you are empty, and drained, and you do not know what you want.

7. Charles Tansley 'felt extremely, even physically, uncomfortable. They were talking about the fishing industry. Why did no one ask him his opinion? What did they know about the fishing industry?'

It behoves the woman, as Lily Briscoe knows, 'whatever her own occupation may be, to go to the help of the young man opposite'. To help him relieve his 'urgent desire to assert himself; as indeed it is their duty to help us, suppose the Tube were to burst into flames'.

'How would it be, she thought, if neither of us did either of these things?'

8. Sometimes I have had to unstitch my work, to say, Oh so you know when I said I was happy to do that? Well, what I meant was the opposite.

9. And so 'she sat there smiling'.

1.   I want to be lying in a field with him, naked, our feet pointing away into the grass. I want to feel the breeze on our bodies. I want to swim in the sea with him. I want his arms around me. I want the sounds of love and desire that he makes.

2.   Mastering abandon, hurtling down the hill in the rickety carriage.

     Mastering myself, not letting anyone else be Lord and Master.

     The master in me, that is us, him, you.

3. He sees me; he has no story. I am not an image of myself, or of him. I am not a tentacle, an extension, a limb. When he reaches out and touches me, it is me – the parts he knows, the parts he does not – that he is reaching out to.

I have no mirror to myself when I am with him. There are no reflections.

I Would Even Say: To Open Her Mouth

1. We argue, one night – we sit on opposite ends of the bed: scowls, raised voices, gesticulations. The bitter side of love, and I feel, my God, can I do this? The time spent unravelling, the time spent restitching. When I want to be here, writing! When I want to be with my words, dipping in and out of Magi, of kings, and streams, dreaming of rivers thick with plants, of bellies filled with fronds. I don't want to be emptying the bins, sifting through, recycling.

   We muddle through to understanding, apology, tenderness. In the morning, we break back into desire. Lying on his chest; his ribs high and wide. Touching him, and then he is touching himself. More firm, and faster, and then I am on my side, and I watch and my breathing is excited, all of me is excited, I love to watch – and then he comes – onto me, my breasts, my belly, my neck.

   I love this. The sudden wet coolness on me. The smell: summer rain on cement. Fresh, open windows.

3. I always liked that – the sharp gasp of wetness on skin.

1. Am I pornography?

1.   It is the end of January. I have been thinking a lot about
      sex. I am in a boxy, grey room in Bloomsbury, early for a
      talk by Shere Hite. I have with me a copy of Virginia
      Woolf's diaries. This, of course, was her stomping-
      ground; after a spell in Richmond, she and Leonard came
      back here in 1924, living at Tavistock Square. Virginia
      used to walk her dog Pinker through the streets; she
      would sit in Gordon Square, 'under the shelter of trees
      with the rain pattering between the leaves', reading, or
      talking with Leonard. I go from office to bookshop, from
      tube to café, drycleaners to library. I walk through these
      two squares, or dip alongside them on my bike, and see
      her there, in a long skirt, a dress – 'I must remember to
      write about my *clothes* next time I have an impulse to
      write. My love of clothes interests me profoundly; only it
      is not love; and what it is I must discover'; 'This is the last
      day of June and finds me in black despair because Clive
      laughed at my new hat' – and I do something, internally,
      halfway between doffing a cap and curtseying. Bowing,
      perhaps. *Un salut bien bas.*

      Woolf's love for Vita Sackville-West flickers throughout
      the diaries. 'Vita having this moment (twenty minutes
      ago) left me, what are my feelings? Of a dim November
      fog; the lights dulled and damped. But this will disperse;
      then I shall want her, clearly and distinctly ...' And then: 'I
      feel a lack of stimulus, of marked days, now Vita is gone;

and some pathos, common to all these partings; and she has four days' journey through the snow.'

After dinner with Lytton Strachey one evening: 'Oh I was right to be in love with him twelve or fifteen years ago.' But her love with Leonard: the sense of a tender, fruitful life together: '... I was overcome with happiness. Then we walked round the square love making – after twenty-five years can't bear to separate. Then I walked round the lake in Regent's Park. Then ... you see it is an enormous pleasure, being wanted: a wife. And our marriage so complete.'

The last entry in her diary reads: 'L. is doing the rhododendrons.'

2.   Shere Hite has much to say about women's relations with men, and women. She comes, escorted, into the room, slightly unsteady on her feet. She has wide, glassy eyes; bleached – flaxen – hair, and an air of confusion and wonder. She doesn't quite seem here; she looks a little plastic, manufactured. Talking in a robotic, trippy monotone, she reads from a paper, pausing at the end of each page for really quite a long time, mid-sentence, to locate the next. The audience is uncomfortable; this is not what we expected. Every now and then she looks up at us, with either a blank look of disorientation or a beatific smile. We shift uneasily in our seats.

In a confusing jangle of thoughts that touch on cloning, romance, brothels, and women loving women, she repeats familiar arguments against the uniformity of the reproductive model of sex; against a sexual culture that prioritizes male orgasm, and that glosses over the fact that few women reach orgasm during penetration.

She is so deeply strange. I have a sudden pang of warmth and gratitude towards her, for it is easy to forget what she did, all those years ago – what all those women did – those women! – I bow to them, hand on heart – again, *un salut bien bas*. I think about pornography's parade of women reaching paroxysms of pleasure through penetrative sex alone; coming crazily, wantonly, easily, through the most perfunctory of attentions from a swollen, mechanical male. For all my feelings that pornography is – of course – a fantasy, a projection of a fear of female sexuality, a way of rendering women as men (and perhaps women?) would like us to be: endlessly affirming a male potency which never fails to bring us to grateful orgasm, I now – oh – feel a cascading dejection at the thought of men, of women, of girls, of boys, thinking that this is what it is like, or what it can only be. Yes yes fuck me there yes yes yeah.

3.   The conversation moves on. Hite is now saying that sex for women has changed; that women are more active in sex; they now have sex on top.

Oh. Oh. I am deflated. Is this all that sexual agency for women might mean? Is power really just that: being on top? And is the converse true: is lack of power being underneath? Gradually, the starkness of her vision – supported by murmuring around me – becomes clear: penetrative sex is unpleasurable, and demeaning. Women, she says, should abandon sex with men, and instead focus on their clitoral pleasure. There is clapping, and there are whooping sounds. I want to growl, in defence of the men who, because they responded to me, because they loved me and wanted me, gave me so much pleasure, so much blurred pleasure – pleasure of a clitoral kind, pleasure of a vaginal kind, pleasure of many kinds, pleasure of who cares what kind?

4.   My irritation builds – she and an audience member are
       agreeing that images of lesbians using dildos in queer
       porn should be boycotted; I become so fidgety I think my
       neighbours will be annoyed, and I wonder if I can leave
       – can I leave? – but I am trapped in the middle of a row,
       and would have to clamber over people sitting in the aisles
       – what a gesture! – to get out, to get some fresh air.

Usually I take issue at this point, and up goes my hand,
and I begin. But today I cannot summon the energy.

I often take issue, but today I am tired, and I have resolved
to write – so I am staying quiet, though I am taking notes
furiously, and my leg is jigging up and down, and a
craving for a cigarette plunges in at me from nowhere.

5.   Sometimes it would be nice, I think – it would be a relief – to be so certain. To be so sure, to have such sharp edges. To know where one began and ended.

But I did, in fact, use to be sure, to be that certain. And it felt like this: like a hard stone in my body that caught and scraped, and made it difficult to move. That made it impossible to feel, to taste and trace the contours of myself, of others.

Today I am tired. I walk out, face burning, into the fresh January night.

1.   I grew up acutely, unhappily, aware of the pull of sex, of what young female bodies could elicit.

I remember standing on a bus, around the age of thirteen, feeling the heavy stare of a sagging, tired man, around the age of my father. It was threaded with hostility; hostility and desire. It wanted me, but it hated me for making that want arise.

I remember, on another bus, a young man groping me. I kicked him. I got off the bus and he chased me down the street. I ran into a shopping centre and lost him.

I remember a pushy older boy at school lifting my skirt up as I passed by with friends. I had a glass of Coke in my hand; I poured it neatly, decisively, over his gelled head.

I remember three drunk, middle-aged men surrounding me in an underground carriage, their acrid, sweaty breath crowding in on me. One of them pinched my fifteen-year-old arse. I raged, and hurled insults at them. My mother told me to be quiet; people would think *I* was the problem.

At university, a drunk interloper I had barely noticed at a party rubbed himself up against me. I pushed him away. As he was manoeuvred out, like an unwieldy sofa, he called me a whore.

2.   I was always aware, I think, of my hunger for men: the sharp arrow of excitement when they walked into a room. Of wanting their hard, uncompromising bodies. Their tough surfaces. Their urgent, wilful desire.

3.   I wanted to plunge into my senses. To bring my body to life!

4.   But these men – these angry, staring men! – the men who want you and then call you a whore.

Court our desire, they say, and we'll use it against you. Provoke a desire that you disappoint, and we will fucking hate you.

5.   It is dangerous to be a girl. Dangerous to be exciting to others. And so, to be *excited*, then – that just adds fuel to the fire. Don't give them more weapons! Don't give them ammunition!

6.   Sometimes, a solution repeats the problem it is designed to resolve.

In the eyes of my culture, I think to myself in my teens, I am a desirable, attracting thing. But I am that: a thing. A plaything. And when that allure, which I have by virtue of being a girl, becomes problematic – when the plaything talks back, or doesn't put out, or does, or kicks you in the shins when you pinch its arse on a bus – then that culture clamps down on that allure, turns it inside out, into whore bitch slut, slut slapper whore.

And so, guilty – excited – lonely – I fashioned a feminism that contained my desire. That kept me safe, and refused to play. That tried to rule against my noisy, volatile self; to put a lid on my hunger.

1. My feminism contained my sexuality, the danger it posed to myself and others, by cloaking it with ambivalence. It allowed my mother and me, in our denouncements of sexist adverts, as we walked arm-in-arm through town, to put the woman that I might become – attractive, attracting, provocative, and therefore both powerful and vulnerable – back into a box.

1. I am singing in a concert at school. I am sixteen; it's summer. I'm talking, laughing with a friend – a handsome, older boy. I feel my grandmother's eyes, watchful, concerned – envious perhaps.

She is gorgeous, and mischievous, and playful.

Her eyes are on me like a slap. I look down, away, caught red-handed, red-faced.

1. Are you a team player?

   Whose side are you on?

2. Get off the pole, you stupid bitch.

3. So, we're all whores now?

4. Silly grown women.

1.   And so I am a knitted, fabric head. I have the appearance
      of having a mouth. But my mouth shuts me in. I am all
      fabric, stitched into myself. I am stuffing cloth into my
      mouth.

1.   We are whispering to each other. Hold my hands down, I
   say.

   We're in the snow, you say. The ice is under your skin,
   your skirts are soaked with cold. I'm dragging you
   through the snow, the woods are all around.

   But of course we're not in the snow, we're right here, right
   here in the warm.

2.   These desires, rioting noisily through me – whose are they?

They are mine, and yours, and everyone else's.

They have found their way inside me, and taken up residence. They have folded their arms, and said, Ha.

Ha.

3. Some wild escape. A lurid, narcotic release – from so much awareness, scrutiny, analysis. The electrifying flip-side of the urge to control, the urge to contain myself.

4.   We are our own archive.

1.   Those hypostasized feminist ancestors – my companions, my people – I see them containing my desire, my perversion. I look over at them, their avid eyes, their conviction. I feel their hands around my throat.

But they are inflatable dolls floating in my memory. Bloated, distended, through accumulation, the distortions of time.

My people – my people! – who showed me the way.

2.   My desire to speak desire, as I struggle against their
     weight, is revisionist: of myself, and of what I understood
     to have made that self. Of the feminism that made me,
     and that forbade my desire; or the feminism I made make
     me – for what makes us choose the canon we choose?

3.   The desire to speak desire is a desire to burst through
     silence, to puncture. As such, it is also erotic; it contains
     its own excitement.

     It undoes the perceived straitjacketing. Unlaces the corset,
     winds down the hair.

[205]

4.   And so these fantasies of submission, abandon, extremity
     – savage, though orchestrated by me – stand hand on hip,
     daring the feminism of my youthful politics to stifle them.
     Daring my ancestors, as they live and breathe within me,
     to hold me down, and cover my mouth.

5.   Just you see, the fantasies say.

     Watch me go, sister.

6.   Ladies and gentlemen of the jury, behold: my own
     feminist erotics, my Russian doll of desire.

7.   Fuck me. Yes, fuck me!

The Desert It Opposes

1. I am at a seminar about pornography. A researcher –
    something of an authority, a spokesperson for re-
    evaluating the politics of pornography research – talks
    about the assumptions wheeled out by anti-pornography
    writers, assumptions that get built into research: that it
    has grown more violent; that young people get their
    'education' about sex from it, and that this is a bad thing.

    He suggests that some of these truisms are wrong. He has
    done extensive research on pornography. He has probably
    watched more pornography than anyone, anywhere.
    Pornography, he says, in fact increases the visibility and
    undoes the stigma of non-normative sexualities and
    bodies: of fat bodies, of hairy bodies, of small bodies, of
    disabled bodies. Pornography is democratic, and
    revealing; it is countering heteronormativity. Pornography
    shows people experiencing pleasure and reaching orgasm.

    Yes!

2.   I can feel the room agreeing with him, wanting to agree with him. I can feel myself wanting to agree with him.

There is something about him that is interesting. He has a quiet swagger. He holds your gaze. He likes being the person he is: the counter-voice; the pornography guy.

Pornography, he says, can be educational, and this can be a good thing. It can show you 'what goes in where'.

Oh. My heart sinks. That feeling, again: wanting to ask a difficult question. I am going to be the one to break the mood; to interrupt that cosy feeling of consensus. The stick-in-the-mud, my brow furrowing.

3.   It is a few months earlier. I am at a talk on pornography at a large feminist gathering. Image after image is shown, the emphasis on violence, on submission, on aggression. The climax is a list of guidelines, a wholesale ruling on the importance of polite, gentle sex within committed relationships, under the sign of romance.

I am with Sarah. We are fidgety, annoyed. I am taking furious notes, furiously. I'm formulating a question. She can sense it. Do it, she says. She is nodding at me. Do it.

I raise my hand. Does the speaker think there is an inherent problem with wanting to look at images of people we find attractive, naked, having sex? Can one really pathologize the experience of the myriads who, whether in a 'romantic relationship' or not, have sex which plays with power, which involves poses and gestures of submission and domination?

The speaker begins to say that, well, she would never judge anyone, but violent sex – and here I interrupt, and say, Well, hang on, who said anything about violent sex? There's a distinction, isn't there, between violence, and consensual play with domination? She looks blank, brushes that aside, and says that some people might find it helpful to join a group such as hers, and learn about feminism.

[214]

She presumes, I notice, that these desires would come out of *not* knowing about feminism; that feminism undoes 'problematic' desires. Whereas we are more than our beliefs. We don't align, neatly, inside ourselves, a stack of equal cards. And since feminism, like anything else, can create its own desires.

But I persevere: Is the only language we have for understanding the complex experiences of pornography, of sex itself, of the many forms it takes, not always in relationships, by people who may even already know about feminism – is the only language we have that of delusion, of ignorance, of collusion?

The speaker is tired of me, I am being difficult. I am not joining in the rally.

Sarah is poking me in the ribs, nodding. A bit later, we leave; we go and drink gin, even though it's mid-afternoon. This was a meeting for feminists, but we feel we have to leave.

4. So, here I am, again. My hand is up. I am asking Mr
    Pornography: Given that for many women, orgasm during
    vaginal sex is elusive, and clitoral stimulation is crucial,
    how then is clitoral pleasure represented in the swathes of
    pornography you have surveyed?

    There is a flicker of unease across his face. He says, in a
    conciliatory way, that it is true that in pornography, for
    every one representation of cunnilingus there are four of
    fellatio.

    He stops there. There is a pause. Oh.

    Right, I go on, So, given your claim that pornography can
    be educational about the mechanics of sex – and I noticed
    you said it can show us 'what goes in where' – doesn't
    that suggest that there is a problem with pornography
    failing to represent the nature, range and realities of
    pleasure in women?

    He seems a bit unsettled. A little bit flummoxed. Well, he
    says, new and emerging forms of pornography – amateur
    pornography, pornography that cuts out the middle man,
    where people turn webcams on themselves and
    masturbate and others tune in and watch – are increasing
    the range of pleasures that people encounter.

Clitoral stimulation as an innovative breakout form! Faint praise, I think to myself, faint fucking praise.

Another silence.

I am expecting him to say more; to address the question; to have a response to something that, surely – surely – someone must have asked him in his years of research.

Nothing comes. I don't want to press the point home – why not, I wonder? Why not make this point more forcefully?

5.   Perhaps I want him to like me. I want, of course, to be good.

Wanting to be good: the opposite of being lucid, the opposite of being active. Wanting to be liked by each in turn.

6.   So I thank him, and hope that this silence, this lack of
      exchange, will have registered, somewhere, in him, in the
      audience.

      But what I want to say is this: the pornography that you
      are arguing can be educational, and represents sex as
      joyful and positive on the basis that it shows people
      experiencing pleasure and reaching orgasm (people who
      are not necessarily experiencing pleasure and who may be
      faking orgasm), and is a liberalizing force in that it
      provides a space for a range of non-normative pleasures,
      is, by your garbled concession, not wholly representing
      women's sexuality, except only through the narrow,
      refracted lens of a prescribed male fantasy: of penis in
      vagina making woman come come come.

7. What's more, praising pornography's 'departures' in this way – the new amateur pornography – without for one moment wondering what that newness tells us, what it takes for granted – takes as a given the shockingly fanciful picture of women's sexuality, and of men's for that matter, that so saturates the kaleidoscope of coming women – yeah yeah yeah! – that we don't even notice it.

   I don't even notice it, when I am in thrall – on the rapid hurtling treadmill – of even a self-consciously feminist pornography that, while – yes – thank goodness – places women's desire centre stage, nonetheless manages to be both coy and brutal. To crown the vaginal orgasm – yeah yeah fuck me yeah! – and to push us, all scrubbed and plucked and bare and clinical, into a glaring hyperactive light.

8. We are women whose bodies can only rage – rage with desire – in response to this sanitized hyperreal.

1. The anti-pornography critique is often ideological and partisan, yes. But what no one in this room can say, what Mr Pornography cannot countenance, is that so too is the defence of pornography, so too is the critique of the critique.

    It too seeks to find evidence for its feeling – in this case, its feeling that pornography has been forbidden, and must be allowed; that sex has been ruled over for too long, and must, finally, be freed.

2. 'We must not think,' says Foucault, 'that by saying yes to sex, one says no to power.'

3.   I want to throw off my fabric-feminism, my stitched-up fabric head. I want to be free!

This desire is so powerful. It's so insanely exciting. And so I too overlook uncomfortable things, things that would counter that desire – because, for me, *this* conflict is the thing I need to resolve. Mr Pornography has something similar but something different he is resolving. Ms Romantic Sex something else again.

4.   In the social world, it is the social that people want. And it is the social that makes our desires: our desires to constrain desire, and to speak desire; to deny desire, and to free desire.

5.   We are all in the same lulling, lurching boat, fashioning our beliefs to resolve our feelings. Paddling frantically to stay afloat.

1. How unpleasant, wrote Woolf, 'to be locked out'. But 'worse perhaps to be locked in'.

2. Here, in these rooms, we have to take sides. If we are liberated, we cannot critique. If we are critical, we cannot enjoy.

3. You may as well tape up my mouth, right now! There is no space to speak.

Left Almost Mute

1. We want to have a story, a position we can hold. A rock we can cling to, a lighthouse we can swim to.

2. There's something I want to tell you, I say.

1.   One August, when I was 24, I trundled off to a Marie
       Stopes clinic in South London. I filled in some forms and
       had my blood taken. The Man I Loved sat in the waiting
       room, unsure what to do – my boyfriend of just a few
       months, with his beautiful face, his shock of Eraserhead
       hair, his crow's-feet smiling eyes. A man I had fallen in
       love with suddenly and deeply, and with whom I had had
       one night of unprotected sex, at a point in my cycle when
       we were sure that it was safe.

2.   Sure that it was safe. I had said those words to a doctor a
       few weeks before, when I had discovered I was pregnant.
       Well, she snapped, you should *never* think that.

4.	After the admin at Marie Stopes, I said goodbye to him;
	he went to work, and I went under, in my green gown.
	Before the wave subsumed me: a hazy doctor and nurse,
	an injection in my arm (or was it a pill?), a counting to ten
	but only getting to three. And then waking up in the ward,
	a surge of nausea, and tears. A nurse turned me onto my
	side, away from the women waiting to go in. And then
	down, down, down, further and further and further I
	tumbled – Alice, pointy boots, tressed hair, topsy turvy
	into a tunnel of grief, into its numbing, invisible embrace.

5.   The following winter I barely went out. I became frightened of dark streets, of being alone. I became near-phobic of anything gory. I cried uncontrollably in concerts and films, switching back into conversation afterwards, a tap turned off.

My throat closed up.

I stopped singing.

6.   One day in the spring I woke up feeling better.
      Unaccountably better, brighter, lighter.

      That's done, I thought.

      I tried to close the door behind me.

7.   But I dreamt of a baby, a soft, real, round baby, whose skin
      I could feel, whose eyelashes fluttered against my cheek in
      the semi-consciousness between wake and sleep.

8.   And then my passions, my ambitions receded. I watched
      them vanish at a dizzying speed.

1. Initially, in that strange, muffled time between deciding and doing, I told a few people. I could feel a ripple of shock and incomprehension, a flicker of anger and disapproval. I had an awkward dinner with one friend; we were, I think, unequipped. How could you be so stupid, I imagine, was the thought that flashed behind the awkwardness. And who knows, perhaps I too would have had the same response? I – who know how babies are made and take contraception into my own hands – I should have known better.

2.   Another friend says she is glad I told her on email.

I am blank in response.

I stitch my mouth up; I say nothing.

3.   Why are mistakes – blunders – so hard to tolerate in others, so hard to tolerate in ourselves?

4.   I was alone, flailing about in the quietness that compressed me, in the blankness with which we all met this moment. We had no words for it, or perhaps no feelings.

What comes first, the feelings or the words?

5.   I remember dancing, together, after realizing, to Jamaican soul, before going to the clinic – to check it was true, to work out what to do. I felt ungraspably happy.

It was summer. His shirt was slightly open. I think he was wearing flip-flops, his grey Muji flip-flops.

6.   Dancing; we did that well. It was where we first found each other, dancing, his hand on my waist.

1. A body – a corpse – my own, I think – wrapped in tape,
    suspended in gaffa. A mummy preserved in an
    underground stasis. My arms taped to my sides, my
    mouth taped over. Tipped over a wall, into a tip.

2. And then underwater, gurgling contorted, undecipherable
    sounds.

3.   Later – years later – I started speaking.

The confession, to a therapist: I threw it up, almost –
shocked at the violence with which it emerged, the
urgency with which it strode onto the stage. I am the star
of this story! Here I am! A child bursting into a room,
confident of its own protagonism.

We'd been doing hypnotherapy, for the shrill, insistent
pain thrumming away just under my skin, all the way
down my spine, hips, legs; for the sensation of something
– a serrated, slightly blunt knife – scraping at me from
just under my surface, from the uppermost edge of
muscle.

I sat bolt upright, disoriented, relieved; something near to
pleasure in the warmth of my tears; ah, yes, of course.
Here it is.

Here it is. Here we are. Here I am.

4.   I made a choice. Right? Right.

I made a decision. *We* made a decision, thinking it is a decision you can make together, that means the same for you both. You think together! You are a collective! You feel together!

Except that you don't, you aren't, you can't.

We made a decision that, at the time, felt right. It turned out to cause me unimaginable pain, a searing sense of loss. But I had no *right* to the torrential unhappiness that threatened to engulf me – because I had made a choice, hadn't I?

5.   You cannot mourn, you cannot claim grief, when you have made a decision. Right?

6.   I don't know. I do not know.

'To this day,' writes Sebald, 'I do not know what to make of such stories.'

1.   I had made my bed. My deathly, guilty bed.

     I hitched up my skirt. I rolled up my sleeves.

2.   In here with you, baby. Cosy little coffin.

1.	Year by year, I undid myself, answering to some deity frowning at me, just out of sight.

	That deity: what was it? A mixture of things: a cultural soup of religions I never shared but was, of course, born into. A discomfort with the body, my unruly, lustful body, its unbridled, guilty febrility. And a profound shame about my terrible mistake: my utter failure of reason.

3.   It wasn't, of course, only a secularist discourse of sin, a moralism about unreason, that bound me up and gagged me. My private, all too private, experience also unfolded in the clunky, riven politics of abortion, where nuance doesn't survive long.

Where you are either with us or against us.

Pro-life or pro-choice.

4. Whose side are you on?

1.   I could have done it in my lunch-break, without an
      anaesthetic – I remember a newspaper article telling me
      that.

      It's just a few tiny cells, someone said. Just the removal of
      a few tiny cells.

      Yes, that's true, of course it is.

      And it is also so much else.

2.   I feel like I've lost something, I kept saying, my head in
      my hands.

3.   I had lost something! A potential child, a potential
      motherhood, with a man I loved, with The Man I Loved.

4.   The Man I Loved!

I used to wish I could draw him, the shape of him that I
loved. There was something of the comic-book about him:
the quiff, the streak of grey, the slightly lopsided stroll.

Those shocking, short-sighted eyes; when he took off his
glasses, they seemed vulnerable, newborn.

5. I had lost something: what could have been; the taste of something new, unfamiliar, intoxicating.

6. The things that were lost!

7.   This broken, bewildered refrain.

    To say it, even just to feel it – it felt like taking sides. A risky concession. An irresponsible betrayal.

10.   The anti-abortion movement spits murderous venom in the name of life. And in the face of sometimes shockingly violent attack – and in order to counter an inflammatory rhetoric about murder – the pro-choice movement has emphasized abortion, or early abortion at least, as a routine, meaningless procedure.

And so we – we women, making our decisions, dealing with the powerful sites that are our bodies as they accompany us, joyously, alarmingly, in our individual lives – we are backed into a corner.

11.   But it is impossible to feel, impossible to grieve, impossible to even know if you are grieving, to know if you have something to grieve, when the hulking monolith of politics looms in, pressing its hands over your mouth, taping it up – or pulling your words out, avid and grasping, wrenching your tongue out with them.

This Savage Place

1. 'Why does one like the frantic, the unmastered?' That is
   Woolf, describing the sea at Cuckmere, the 'great spray
   fountain bursting to my joy over the parade and the
   lighthouse. Right over the car'.

2. The sea: the space that I watch from a window; excited,
   alarmed by the swell, the splash, the depths.

3.   The strange distorted joy that comes from being near something deathly, from looking over the abyss, and recovering ground.

It's close to excitement, and it's close to relief.

Ah yes, this.

This.

1.	There were moments of light.

	Rachel and I pulled up weeds and grew vegetables in a hot, playful garden. The courgettes were luminous, pale green, with corrugated surfaces. Cut them up into earthy, pastel stars. They were sweet and moist and crunchy.

2.	Lying in a taxi, on the way to a doctor, watching the leaves on the trees go by, upside down, in their spring shimmering. A wave of joy: I could be out of all this – I could be free! But the light closed back in on itself, a shell snapping shut.

3.   I could dance; I danced.

We had parties. We drank gin, and lay in the grass under
the stars. I didn't talk much; or rather, I talked, but did not
really speak.

4.   It was there, dancing – hips free, body unlocked – that I
could touch abandon, that I could taste pleasure again.
And it was there that I could almost crash through myself.
Dancing a death dance. In a little Joy Division of my own.

5. Years later, I roamed, stunned, excited, through the Neues Museum in Berlin: rebuilt, restored; the archive of itself.

Its wounds preserved, lovingly rendered. Its memory on its skin.

6. Falling asleep: pulling up the bindweed, following it round the garden. So strong, so thick; a faultline, stuff of the earth. The relief when you reach its root and yank it out. Seeing the trace in the crumbly soil where you followed its determined, fibrous journey.

7. A bird led me out of a dense, brambly wood. It led me with twine, some thick dark rope.

    Knotty, vegetal, fleshy.

So Full Of Sleep

1. Low in affect, drugged in love.

   Slow in movement, slurred of voice.

   Hypnotic.

   Alcoholic.

   A record slowed down.

2.   It has rained, freezing rain, over snow – the town now an
      ice rink of risk.

      Something catches my eye on the pavement: a jumper,
      trapped under ice, arms in a pose of readiness. A cartoon
      character, Popeye, a cliché of decisiveness. About to
      sprint, but frozen. Trapped rigid, under ice.

3.   There are many beginnings. There are so many stories. But after the abortion, I just stopped living, and in the end – in this end – that's what seeded my pain, and that's what broke our love. It couldn't be let in to the fluid waters; couldn't be dissolved into the stream. Already our past was too heavy, and we slowly, reluctantly buckled.

1. But then if he hadn't been so stuck – so hesitant – so absent from himself, and also then from me, from us – if he had been more embracing of life, of his own life and of ours, then perhaps my grief would not have thrived, would not have grown so hungrily. Perhaps we could have addressed it, and written over it with love.

2.　　I stitched my desire up.

My desire for us, for a future together. I knitted it into my mouth, where it coated the wet place of my voice.

And when I tried to unravel it, he froze – the stiffness in his torso tightening.

Or he just fell asleep. The sleep of the dead.

3.   I was a bird at the window, tapping my beak on the glass.

4. Peck peck!

    Peck peck!

5.   Till my fucking head hurt, till the scenery swam, till my teeth loosened in my jaw.

1.   I wanted more – more from him, more than him.

     I wanted to fill myself with life, fill myself with my life.

     I wanted more – more – more life!

2. I'd been mistaking death for life, mistaking poison for food.

I'd been taking the leg. Sitting, too long, in the draught.

I'd been so good, so good at being good.

3.   It's hard to want more, to be more, than a man.

      I didn't want to want more, to be more, than a man – than
      my man, than this man, than The Man.

4.   Let the boy win at tennis!

5.   To him, then, to the Man I Loved, to my own personal Magus, the pain said: I want so much more, but I am not going anywhere. I shall not show you up with my life. I shall take a scythe to myself. I shall hack at my roots. And I shall keep you company.

1.   The pain, the pain. That searing, fucking pain.

I couldn't believe no one else could hear it! Its drumming, its droning, its screeching. It elbowed everything out of the way, and took centre stage, triumphant.

Leering, in its heavy army boots. Its armour clunking. Its eyes wild, hair matted.

2. And so, in the end – in this end – the pain was a solution: a bird killed with one stone. A solution to my fear that if my body were fluid, were full of its joyous, pressing life, full of my life – my dreaming, driven life – then I would outstrip him, and outstrip this love. I would grow my limbs back, and stop dreaming of amputation. I would push up through the soil, wiping the dirt from my face, shaking the worms from my hair. And I would clamber over us, and be large and long and wild and free.

1. I didn't, of course, know any of this then – or not in the way that I know it now. 'A person,' writes Jonathan Lear, 'is, by his nature, out of touch with his own subjectivity. One cannot find out what it is like for a person to be just by asking. Even if he is sincere, he won't know the answer.'

1. I found a fox – not caught by dogs – perhaps hit by a car. But intact, beautifully, shockingly intact. I could see no blood, no wound. He lay there, on his side, on the southern underbelly of Peckham Rye, a restful body of red, a serene splash of white. It seemed as if someone had laid him down there, with love. I stayed a long time. He looked almost asleep; I thought perhaps I could see his belly rising and falling, but no. I didn't take him in my hands; I didn't feel his little heart, beating so fast. Everything was so quiet, watching him there; everything became noiseless and still.

1.   We lie side by side, The Man I Loved and I, in the busy
      London night.

      Something shifts queasily inside me. A sickly cog turns.

2.   'Strength,' wrote Sontag, 'is what I want.' Strength to act.
      'Not to endure, I have that and it has made me weak.'

3.   I go to the British Museum and see the horses we stole
from the Greeks – bursting through the stone,
Michelangelo's slaves. I can feel the wind shaking their
manes. I can hear the horsemen's shouts. I can smell the
creatures, I can hear their hooves. I can feel the air
snorting from their dilated nostrils.

The blood pulses through their veined, straining bellies.

Their eyes are gleaming.

4.   And then one day, it comes; I say it.

     I've said it before, usually in night rages, after which
     daytime and love come flooding up, and wash the truth
     away.

     But something, this time, cuts through everything else.
     My words are a newly sharpened knife: pleasing,
     alarming, swift.

5.   The blood oozes, thick, slow, drunk.

1. It was strange and exquisite: the clarity, the release. Cool liquid morphine, a drip in the hospital.

2. The loss, too, was sharp and clear. As piercing and painful as light.

3.　　I hadn't wanted this to end. More than anything, I had wanted it to work; to let our bodies do their beautiful, complex thing; to let our love stretch out into the hills.

More than anything.

And so of course it had to end. In order to live, I had to let it die.

4.　　No crumpling of limbs, just a silent, sideways keel.

1. In those first few months apart, we spent a day at the Notting Hill Carnival. We walked through the streets, and found a green circled by stalls. We danced, bobbed, slowly, in the lowering sun.

That was how we had begun, all those years ago: dancing, to Sinatra I think, our strangers' bodies close. There had been a lot of dancing. Mostly, we danced separately, facing each other, not touching. I only remember dancing together, our bodies together, at the very beginning, and at the very end.

Harnessed To A Shark

1. True stories, false stories; half stories, whole stories. Old stories, new stories. Death stories, life stories.

2. I could tell other stories. There are so many stories!

   But it is this story, its warm generous body, that is the freedom from it.

   It's the story that changed the story.

1. Crossing Waterloo Bridge, that spritely spring, that razor-sharp spring, looking over at St Paul's, I sniffed pleasure – openness – light – in the air.

    I could feel it in my hips.

1. One bright morning, we lie in the bath – the windows open – the breeze, the space, so free. Outside, the crows are squawking. An occasional siren unzips the air.

    We lie in the bath and sing. I do my best Elvis, via Sarah Vaughan. There Will Be Peace In The Valley.

    Peace in the valley, for me, someday.

2. It's like we are on holiday, we say. A summer holiday, in the bath!

3. I wonder: if a man – if My Man, if The Man – were enough, were big enough to contain me, for me to feel contained in him, in his largeness, the largeness of his person – would I need him to tie me up?

    Would I need him to tie me down?

4. Would I need to take the sting out of myself?

5. 'To write,' said Sontag, 'you have to allow yourself to be the person you don't want to be (of all the people you are).'

6. To write, she said, 'I have to be lucid, alone.'

1. I love to feel him behind me, when he has me in his grip, and I feel that I am at his mercy, even if I'm not, because my desire, for all its histories, is right here – is centre-stage, and he loves my desire, its folded depths, its hurtling tunnels, its sharp, painful edges; and I know that we could stop at any moment, and I feel the warm, large shelter of our love around us; a shelter that holds within it the scarves around my ankles, the sound of his voice as he sings in the kitchen, his ability to see me and hear me and just let me be; our feet touching as we lie, quiet, in the sun, reading, breathing.

2.   Now, though, we are far from home. We have woken early
      with jetlag, with the sirens outside, the clatter of the city
      cranking itself into the day. He is behind me, and then I
      am above him, and we have slid off the bed onto the floor,
      where a mirror watches us. I can see us, he cannot – there
      is something in the way.

      After the madness, when I have felt his claws on my skin,
      and I have bitten back, I rest my head on his shoulder.
      You are gorgeous, we say, and I love you.

3.   Later, I will be on a train edging north, the minor sixth of its horn mourning its way along the Hudson. And then I will be on a plane, travelling west. I will be six thousand miles away: a continent and a sea away.

On the train, everything rattles, and the carriage lurches violently. But all is still, exceedingly quiet. I feel the blood in me. I feel my veins.

5.   Here, now, outside a fruit shop, in the suddenly humid day, we kiss, and the world recedes. All there is is this: his mouth, his body against mine, his tongue playing and probing, his lip under my teeth. I drop my bag to the ground. We are rushing into the tunnel, we are falling into the well.

I could just unpeel him right here. I could just do that, right now.

Notes and Acknowledgements

The subtitle of the book uses a phrase from Michel Foucault, *The History of Sexuality, Volume 1: The Will to Knowledge* (Allen Lane, 1979, first published in 1976 as *Histoire de la Sexualité: La Volonté de Savoir*, Gallimard): One 'goes about telling, with the greatest precision, whatever is most difficult to tell'.

To Spend Oneself, To Gamble Oneself

This section title is taken from Susan Sontag, *Reborn: Early Diaries, 1947–1963*, ed. David Rieff (Hamish Hamilton, 2009), entry for 19 November 1959.

V, 1: The words by Virginia Woolf are from 'Professions for Women', a lecture to the National Society for Women's Service delivered on 21 January 1931. From *The Crowded Dance of Modern Life*, ed. Rachel Bowlby (Penguin, 1993).

V, 2: This incorporates phrases from Sontag, *Reborn* (all remaining Sontag material is from this book): 21 January 1960; undated, February 1960.

V, 3: This is from Virginia Woolf's *Selected Diaries*, ed. A. O. Bell, (Vintage, 2008), 5 February 1935.

Words Words Words: Or, To Marry A King?

This section title draws on a phrase from Carolyn Steedman (which I make use of later also, in *II, 5.*), *Landscape for a Good Woman: A Story of Two Lives* (Virago, 1986).

I, 4 & 5 similarly incorporate material from Steedman, *Landscape for a Good Woman*.

II, 2: The Susie Orbach material is from *Fat is a Feminist Issue* (Paddington Press, 1978).

II, 6: This draws on Sontag, *Reborn*, 26 March 1963.

IV, 2: The Havelock Ellis material can be found in *Studies in the Psychology of Sex*, Volume VI: *Sex in Relation to Society* (F. A. Davis & Co., 1928).

V, 7 & 8: These incorporate material from Milan Kundera, *The Unbearable Lightness of Being* (Faber, 1984).

VIII, 5: Sontag, *Reborn*, 14–15 September 1961.

VIII, 7: This draws on phrases from Shunryu Suzuki, *Zen Mind, Beginner's Mind: Informal talks on Zen Meditation and Practice* (Weatherhill, 1970).

IX, 3: Sontag, *Reborn*, 14 July 1958; 15 September 1962.

IX, 4: Sontag, *Reborn*, 12 June 1961.

IX, 5: Sontag, *Reborn*, undated, February 1960.

IX, 6: This takes up a phrase quoted by Susie Orbach in *Fat is a Feminist Issue*.

X, 2: This incorporates material from Virginia Woolf's *To the Lighthouse* (Hogarth Press, 1927).

(The Skill First) To Make Her Desire

This section title draws on Havelock Ellis's citation of Balzac (*Physiologie du Mariage*) in Ellis's *Studies in the Psychology of Sex*, Volume VI: *Sex in Relation to Society*: 'A man must never permit himself a pleasure with his wife which he has not the skill first to make her desire.'

II, 3: The Virginia Woolf quote is from *A Room of One's Own* (Hogarth Press, 1928).

III, 2: Sontag, *Reborn*, undated, autumn 1959.

More Gone

This section title draws on Sontag, *Reborn*, 12 June 1959, and it recurs in *I, 3*.

III, 3: 'An attenuated hungry voice' reworks a phrase from Sally Alexander, 'Women, Class and Sexual Differences in the 1830s and 1840s: Some Reflections on the Writing of a Feminist History', *History Workshop Journal*, 1984, 17(1), 125–49.

Safe Words: Or, Quickly, Kindly

The second part of this section title draws on a phrase from Woolf, *To the Lighthouse*.

I, 1: The material by Michel Foucault is from *History of Sexuality*, Volume 1: *The Will to Knowledge*.

III, 3: This makes use of a phrase from Sontag, *Reborn*, 14 July 1958.

III, 7 & 9: The Virginia Woolf material is from *To the Lighthouse*.

I Would Even Say: To Open Her Mouth

This section title draws on Helène Cixous, *Le Rire de la Méduse et Autres Ironies* (Galilée, 2010).

III, 1: This section includes phrases from Virginia Woolf's *Diaries*: 11 July 1927; 14 May 1925; 30 June 1926; 19 January 1926; 17 October 1924; 22 October, 1937; 24 March 1941.

IX, 2: 'Some wild escape' recalls words spoken by Tracey Emin in her 1995 film *Why I Never Became a Dancer*.

The Desert It Opposes

This section title recalls Italo Calvino, *Invisible Cities* (Vintage, 1997, first published in 1972): 'Each city receives its form from the desert it opposes; and so the camel driver and the sailor see Despina, a border city between two deserts.'

II, 2: The Michel Foucault quote is from *History of Sexuality*, Volume 1.

III, 1: Virginia Woolf's words are in *A Room of One's Own*.

Left Almost Mute

This section title makes use of a phrase in a letter by psychoanalyst Robert Stoller to psychiatrist Ann Chappell, 27 July 1977: 'Your recent letters raise important, painful, and difficult problems ... and I am left almost mute because so many major issues are involved.' American Psychiatric Association archival materials, Box 100904.

IV, 1: This section draws on the phrase 'Suspended in Gaffa', from Kate Bush's song of that name on *The Dreaming* (1982).

IV, 6: W. G. Sebald's words are from *The Rings of Saturn* (Harvill Press, 1998).

This Savage Place

This title is from Dante's *Divine Comedy: Inferno*, Canto 1, trans. John D. Sinclair (Oxford University Press, 1939).

II, 1: This makes use of words from Woolf's *Diaries*, 25 October 1937. She also describes this scene in a letter to Ethel Smyth, written the day after the diary entry.

II, 4: This draws on lyrics from The Smiths' 'Sweet and Tender Hooligan', from *Louder Than Bombs* (1987).

So Full Of Sleep

This section title is from Dante's *Inferno*, again from Canto I.

IV, 3: Sontag, *Reborn*, 13–14 April 1961.

V, 1: This comes from Jonathan Lear's *Love and its Place in Nature: A Philosophical Interpretation of Freudian Psychoanalysis* (Farrar, Straus & Giroux, 1990).

VI, 1: This section plays with phrases from Kate Bush's 'Hounds of Love', from the album of that name (1985).

VII, 2: This is a rendering of Sontag, *Reborn*, undated, early 1958.

Harnessed To A Shark

This section title refers to a phrase in Virginia Woolf's *Diaries*, 27 October 1935.

III, 1: The song is by Thomas A. Dorsey (1937), recorded by Elvis Presley in 1957.

III, 5 & 6: Sontag, *Reborn*, 13 August 1961; 12 June 1961.

IV, 4: This makes use of words from Michel Foucault, 'Truth, Power, Self', a 1982 interview in *Technologies of the Self: A Seminar with Michel Foucault*, ed. Luther H. Martin, Huck Gutman, Patrick H. Hutton (University of Massachusetts Press, 1988).

Thanks

First and foremost, I would like to thank Sarah Chalfant at the
Wylie Agency. Her deep understanding and commitment
enabled me to write the book I most wanted to write, and I am
profoundly grateful to her. Likewise, I am profoundly grateful to
Helen Conford and Stefan McGrath at Penguin/Allen Lane. It
has been a privilege and a pleasure to be published by them.
Helen's editorial prowess has been awe-inspiring, and this book
is all the better for it. Many thanks too to Richard Duguid, Maria
Garbutt-Lucero, Patrick Loughran, and Claire Mason at Penguin,
and to Alba Ziegler-Bailey at the Wylie Agency, for all their work
on the book. The following people, in one way or another, also
helped the book emerge: Oliver Burkeman, John Constable, John
Cornwell, Adam Foulds, John Forrester, John Freeman, Robin
Harvie, Sarah Hodges, Claudia Stein, Mathew Thomson, and
Anna Webber. Others have helped me stay the course: Feona
Attwood, Meg Barker, Alex Dymock, Sara Holloway, Kate Mayne,
Michal Shavit and Cecilia Sosa. I am grateful to them all – as I
am to Nick Blackburn, Sam Byers, Allie Carr, Christen Clifford,
Sophie Collins, Richard Dodwell, Lauren Elkin, Jean Hannah
Edelstein, Chris Goode, David Hayden, Clara Perez, Cassie
Robinson, Isabelle Schoelcher, and Kate Zambreno, for support,
companionship, and collaboration of many wonderful kinds.
Crucial to everything were Charles Buchan and Sarah Chew. I

want to thank my tremendous family, Ros, David, and Mitzi Angel – for so much. And deep thanks – for more than I can fathom – to Miriam Leonard, Patrick Mackie, Sasha Mudd, Mauricio Sierra, and Rachel Warrington.

ALLEN LANE
an imprint of
PENGUIN BOOKS

Recently Published

Mark Greengrass, *Christendom Destroyed: Europe 1517-1650*

Hugh Thomas, *World Without End: The Global Empire of Philip II*

Richard Layard and David M. Clark, *Thrive: The Power of Evidence-Based Psychological Therapies*

Uwe Tellkamp, *The Tower: A Novel*

Zelda la Grange, *Good Morning, Mr Mandela*

Ahron Bregman, *Cursed Victory: A History of Israel and the Occupied Territories*

Tristram Hunt, *Ten Cities that Made an Empire*

Jordan Ellenberg, *How Not to Be Wrong: The Power of Mathematical Thinking*

David Marquand, *Mammon's Kingdom: An Essay on Britain, Now*

Justin Marozzi, *Baghdad: City of Peace, City of Blood*

Adam Tooze, *The Deluge: The Great War and the Remaking of Global Order 1916-1931*

John Micklethwait and Adrian Wooldridge, *The Fourth Revolution: The Global Race to Reinvent the State*

Steven D. Levitt and Stephen J. Dubner, *Think Like a Freak: How to Solve Problems, Win Fights and Be a Slightly Better Person*

Alexander Monro, *The Paper Trail: An Unexpected History of the World's Greatest Invention*

Jacob Soll, *The Reckoning: Financial Accountability and the Making and Breaking of Nations*

Gerd Gigerenzer, *Risk Savvy: How to Make Good Decisions*

James Lovelock, *A Rough Ride to the Future*

Michael Lewis, *Flash Boys*

Hans Ulrich Obrist, *Ways of Curating*

Mai Jia, *Decoded: A Novel*

Richard Mabey, *Dreams of the Good Life: The Life of Flora Thompson and the Creation of* Lark Rise to Candleford

Danny Dorling, *All That Is Solid: The Great Housing Disaster*

Leonard Susskind and Art Friedman, *Quantum Mechanics: The Theoretical Minimum*

Michio Kaku, *The Future of the Mind: The Scientific Quest to Understand, Enhance and Empower the Mind*

Nicholas Epley, *Mindwise: How we Understand what others Think, Believe, Feel and Want*

Geoff Dyer, *Contest of the Century: The New Era of Competition with China*

Yaron Matras, *I Met Lucky People: The Story of the Romani Gypsies*

Larry Siedentop, *Inventing the Individual: The Origins of Western Liberalism*

Dick Swaab, *We Are Our Brains: A Neurobiography of the Brain, from the Womb to Alzheimer's*

Max Tegmark, *Our Mathematical Universe: My Quest for the Ultimate Nature of Reality*

David Pilling, *Bending Adversity: Japan and the Art of Survival*

Hooman Majd, *The Ministry of Guidance Invites You to Not Stay: An American Family in Iran*

Roger Knight, *Britain Against Napoleon: The Organisation of Victory, 1793-1815*

Alan Greenspan, *The Map and the Territory: Risk, Human Nature and the Future of Forecasting*

Daniel Lieberman, *Story of the Human Body: Evolution, Health and Disease*

Malcolm Gladwell, *David and Goliath: Underdogs, Misfits and the Art of Battling Giants*

Paul Collier, *Exodus: Immigration and Multiculturalism in the 21st Century*

John Eliot Gardiner, *Music in the Castle of Heaven: Immigration and Multiculturalism in the 21st Century*

Catherine Merridale, *Red Fortress: The Secret Heart of Russia's History*

Ramachandra Guha, *Gandhi Before India*

Vic Gatrell, *The First Bohemians: Life and Art in London's Golden Age*

Richard Overy, *The Bombing War: Europe 1939-1945*

Charles Townshend, *The Republic: The Fight for Irish Independence, 1918-1923*

Eric Schlosser, *Command and Control*

Sudhir Venkatesh, *Floating City: Hustlers, Strivers, Dealers, Call Girls and Other Lives in Illicit New York*

Sendhil Mullainathan and Eldar Shafir, *Scarcity: Why Having Too Little Means So Much*

John Drury, *Music at Midnight: The Life and Poetry of George Herbert*

Philip Coggan, *The Last Vote: The Threats to Western Democracy*

Richard Barber, *Edward III and the Triumph of England*

Daniel M Davis, *The Compatibility Gene*

John Bradshaw, *Cat Sense: The Feline Enigma Revealed*

Roger Knight, *Britain Against Napoleon: The Organisation of Victory, 1793-1815*

Thurston Clarke, *JFK's Last Hundred Days: An Intimate Portrait of a Great President*

Jean Drèze and Amartya Sen, *An Uncertain Glory: India and its Contradictions*

Rana Mitter, *China's War with Japan, 1937-1945: The Struggle for Survival*

Tom Burns, *Our Necessary Shadow: The Nature and Meaning of Psychiatry*

Sylvain Tesson, *Consolations of the Forest: Alone in a Cabin in the Middle Taiga*

George Monbiot, *Feral: Searching for Enchantment on the Frontiers of Rewilding*

Ken Robinson and Lou Aronica, *Finding Your Element: How to Discover Your Talents and Passions and Transform Your Life*

David Stuckler and Sanjay Basu, *The Body Economic: Why Austerity Kills*

Suzanne Corkin, *Permanent Present Tense: The Man with No Memory, and What He Taught the World*

Daniel C. Dennett, *Intuition Pumps and Other Tools for Thinking*

Adrian Raine, *The Anatomy of Violence: The Biological Roots of Crime*

Eduardo Galeano, *Children of the Days: A Calendar of Human History*

Lee Smolin, *Time Reborn: From the Crisis of Physics to the Future of the Universe*

Michael Pollan, *Cooked: A Natural History of Transformation*

David Graeber, *The Democracy Project: A History, a Crisis, a Movement*

Brendan Simms, *Europe: The Struggle for Supremacy, 1453 to the Present*

Oliver Bullough, *The Last Man in Russia and the Struggle to Save a Dying Nation*

Diarmaid MacCulloch, *Silence: A Christian History*

Evgeny Morozov, *To Save Everything, Click Here: Technology, Solutionism, and the Urge to Fix Problems that Don't Exist*

David Cannadine, *The Undivided Past: History Beyond Our Differences*

Michael Axworthy, *Revolutionary Iran: A History of the Islamic Republic*

Jaron Lanier, *Who Owns the Future?*

John Gray, *The Silence of Animals: On Progress and Other Modern Myths*

Paul Kildea, *Benjamin Britten: A Life in the Twentieth Century*

Jared Diamond, *The World Until Yesterday: What Can We Learn from Traditional Societies?*

Nassim Nicholas Taleb, *Antifragile: How to Live in a World We Don't Understand*

Alan Ryan, *On Politics: A History of Political Thought from Herodotus to the Present*

Roberto Calasso, *La Folie Baudelaire*

Carolyn Abbate and Roger Parker, *A History of Opera: The Last Four Hundred Years*

Yang Jisheng, *Tombstone: The Untold Story of Mao's Great Famine*

Caleb Scharf, *Gravity's Engines: The Other Side of Black Holes*

Jancis Robinson, Julia Harding and José Vouillamoz, *Wine Grapes: A Complete Guide to 1,368 Vine Varieties, including their Origins and Flavours*

David Bownes, Oliver Green and Sam Mullins, *Underground: How the Tube Shaped London*

Niall Ferguson, *The Great Degeneration: How Institutions Decay and Economies Die*

Chrystia Freeland, *Plutocrats: The Rise of the New Global Super-Rich*

David Thomson, *The Big Screen: The Story of the Movies and What They Did to Us*

Halik Kochanski, *The Eagle Unbowed: Poland and the Poles in the Second World War*

Kofi Annan with Nader Mousavizadeh, *Interventions: A Life in War and Peace*

Mark Mazower, *Governing the World: The History of an Idea*

Anne Applebaum, *Iron Curtain: The Crushing of Eastern Europe 1944-56*

Steven Johnson, *Future Perfect: The Case for Progress in a Networked Age*

Christopher Clark, *The Sleepwalkers: How Europe Went to War in 1914*

Neil MacGregor, *Shakespeare's Restless World*

Nate Silver, *The Signal and the Noise: The Art and Science of Prediction*

Chinua Achebe, *There Was a Country: A Personal History of Biafra*

John Darwin, *Unfinished Empire: The Global Expansion of Britain*

Jerry Brotton, *A History of the World in Twelve Maps*

Patrick Hennessey, *KANDAK: Fighting with Afghans*

Katherine Angel, *Unmastered: A Book on Desire, Most Difficult to Tell*

David Priestland, *Merchant, Soldier, Sage: A New History of Power*

Stephen Alford, *The Watchers: A Secret History of the Reign of Elizabeth I*

Tom Feiling, *Short Walks from Bogotá: Journeys in the New Colombia*

Pankaj Mishra, *From the Ruins of Empire: The Revolt Against the West and the Remaking of Asia*

Geza Vermes, *Christian Beginnings: From Nazareth to Nicaea, AD 30-325*

Steve Coll, *Private Empire: ExxonMobil and American Power*

Joseph Stiglitz, *The Price of Inequality*

Dambisa Moyo, *Winner Take All: China's Race for Resources and What it Means for Us*

Robert Skidelsky and Edward Skidelsky, *How Much is Enough? The Love of Money, and the Case for the Good Life*

Frances Ashcroft, *The Spark of Life: Electricity in the Human Body*

Sebastian Seung, *Connectome: How the Brain's Wiring Makes Us Who We Are*

Callum Roberts, *Ocean of Life*

Orlando Figes, *Just Send Me Word: A True Story of Love and Survival in the Gulag*

Leonard Mlodinow, *Subliminal: The Revolution of the New Unconscious and What it Teaches Us about Ourselves*

John Romer, *A History of Ancient Egypt: From the First Farmers to the Great Pyramid*

Ruchir Sharma, *Breakout Nations: In Pursuit of the Next Economic Miracle*

Michael J. Sandel, *What Money Can't Buy: The Moral Limits of Markets*

Dominic Sandbrook, *Seasons in the Sun: The Battle for Britain, 1974-1979*

Tariq Ramadan, *The Arab Awakening: Islam and the New Middle East*

Jonathan Haidt, *The Righteous Mind: Why Good People are Divided by Politics and Religion*

Ahmed Rashid, *Pakistan on the Brink: The Future of Pakistan, Afghanistan and the West*

Tim Weiner, *Enemies: A History of the FBI*

Mark Pagel, *Wired for Culture: The Natural History of Human Cooperation*

George Dyson, *Turing's Cathedral: The Origins of the Digital Universe*

Cullen Murphy, *God's Jury: The Inquisition and the Making of the Modern World*

Richard Sennett, *Together: The Rituals, Pleasures and Politics of Co-operation*

Faramerz Dabhoiwala, *The Origins of Sex: A History of the First Sexual Revolution*

Roy F. Baumeister and John Tierney, *Willpower: Rediscovering Our Greatest Strength*

Jesse J. Prinz, *Beyond Human Nature: How Culture and Experience Shape Our Lives*

Robert Holland, *Blue-Water Empire: The British in the Mediterranean since 1800*

Jodi Kantor, *The Obamas: A Mission, A Marriage*

Philip Coggan, *Paper Promises: Money, Debt and the New World Order*

Charles Nicholl, *Traces Remain: Essays and Explorations*

Daniel Kahneman, *Thinking, Fast and Slow*

Hunter S. Thompson, *Fear and Loathing at* Rolling Stone*: The Essential Writing of Hunter S. Thompson*

Duncan Campbell-Smith, *Masters of the Post: The Authorized History of the Royal Mail*

Colin McEvedy, *Cities of the Classical World: An Atlas and Gazetteer of 120 Centres of Ancient Civilization*

Heike B. Görtemaker, *Eva Braun: Life with Hitler*

Brian Cox and Jeff Forshaw, *The Quantum Universe: Everything that Can Happen Does Happen*

Nathan D. Wolfe, *The Viral Storm: The Dawn of a New Pandemic Age*

Norman Davies, *Vanished Kingdoms: The History of Half-Forgotten Europe*

Michael Lewis, *Boomerang: The Meltdown Tour*

Steven Pinker, *The Better Angels of Our Nature: The Decline of Violence in History and Its Causes*

Robert Trivers, *Deceit and Self-Deception: Fooling Yourself the Better to Fool Others*

Thomas Penn, *Winter King: The Dawn of Tudor England*

Daniel Yergin, *The Quest: Energy, Security and the Remaking of the Modern World*

Michael Moore, *Here Comes Trouble: Stories from My Life*

Ali Soufan, *The Black Banners: Inside the Hunt for Al Qaeda*

Jason Burke, *The 9/11 Wars*

Timothy D. Wilson, *Redirect: The Surprising New Science of Psychological Change*

Ian Kershaw, *The End: Hitler's Germany, 1944-45*

T M Devine, *To the Ends of the Earth: Scotland's Global Diaspora, 1750-2010*

Catherine Hakim, *Honey Money: The Power of Erotic Capital*

Douglas Edwards, *I'm Feeling Lucky: The Confessions of Google Employee Number 59*

John Bradshaw, *In Defence of Dogs*

Chris Stringer, *The Origin of Our Species*

Lila Azam Zanganeh, *The Enchanter: Nabokov and Happiness*

David Stevenson, *With Our Backs to the Wall: Victory and Defeat in 1918*

Evelyn Juers, *House of Exile: War, Love and Literature, from Berlin to Los Angeles*

Henry Kissinger, *On China*

Michio Kaku, *Physics of the Future: How Science Will Shape Human Destiny and Our Daily Lives by the Year 2100*

David Abulafia, *The Great Sea: A Human History of the Mediterranean*

John Gribbin, *The Reason Why: The Miracle of Life on Earth*

Anatol Lieven, *Pakistan: A Hard Country*

William Cohen, *Money and Power: How Goldman Sachs Came to Rule the World*

Joshua Foer, *Moonwalking with Einstein: The Art and Science of Remembering Everything*

Simon Baron-Cohen, *Zero Degrees of Empathy: A New Theory of Human Cruelty*

Manning Marable, *Malcolm X: A Life of Reinvention*

David Deutsch, *The Beginning of Infinity: Explanations that Transform the World*

David Edgerton, *Britain's War Machine: Weapons, Resources and Experts in the Second World War*

John Kasarda and Greg Lindsay, *Aerotropolis: The Way We'll Live Next*

David Gilmour, *The Pursuit of Italy: A History of a Land, Its Regions and Their Peoples*

Niall Ferguson, *Civilization: The West and the Rest*

Tim Flannery, *Here on Earth: A New Beginning*

Robert Bickers, *The Scramble for China: Foreign Devils in the Qing Empire, 1832-1914*

Mark Malloch-Brown, *The Unfinished Global Revolution: The Limits of Nations and the Pursuit of a New Politics*

King Abdullah of Jordan, *Our Last Best Chance: The Pursuit of Peace in a Time of Peril*

Eliza Griswold, *The Tenth Parallel: Dispatches from the Faultline between Christianity and Islam*

Brian Greene, *The Hidden Reality: Parallel Universes and the Deep Laws of the Cosmos*

John Gray, *The Immortalization Commission: The Strange Quest to Cheat Death*

Patrick French, *India: A Portrait*

Lizzie Collingham, *The Taste of War: World War Two and the Battle for Food*

Hooman Majd, *The Ayatollahs' Democracy: An Iranian Challenge*

Dambisa Moyo, *How The West Was Lost: Fifty Years of Economic Folly - and the Stark Choices Ahead*

Evgeny Morozov, *The Net Delusion: How Not to Liberate the World*

Ron Chernow, *Washington: A Life*

Nassim Nicholas Taleb, *The Bed of Procrustes: Philosophical and Practical Aphorisms*

Hugh Thomas, *The Golden Age: The Spanish Empire of Charles V*

Amanda Foreman, *A World on Fire: An Epic History of Two Nations Divided*

Nicholas Ostler, *The Last Lingua Franca: English until the Return of Babel*

Richard Miles, *Ancient Worlds: The Search for the Origins of Western Civilization*

Neil MacGregor, *A History of the World in 100 Objects*

Steven Johnson, *Where Good Ideas Come From: The Natural History of Innovation*

Dominic Sandbrook, *State of Emergency: The Way We Were: Britain, 1970-1974*

Jim Al-Khalili, *Pathfinders: The Golden Age of Arabic Science*

Ha-Joon Chang, *23 Things They Don't Tell You About Capitalism*

Robin Fleming, *Britain After Rome: The Fall and Rise, 400 to 1070*